SILENT SOLITUDES
A Collection of Poetical Thoughts

ABOUT THE AUTHOR

Tony Stringfellow was born and educated in Wolverhampton, attending St. Chad's Grammar School. A well-known and respected artist/sculptor, working in the entertainment business for over 20 years. He has written books, many short stories and articles, and has been writing poetry since he was 13 years old, now also writing and directing for his own production company. He now lives with his family in Shropshire.

www.tonystringfellow.com

SILENT SOLITUDES

A Collection of Poetical Thoughts.
By
Tony Stringfellow

Breeze Hayward Publishing

First Published 2007

Tony Stringfellow has asserted the Author's right under the Copyright, Designs and patents act 1988 to be identified as the Author of this work

ISBN 978-0-9555549-1-9

A catalogue record of this book is registered at the British Library.

Published by Breeze Hayward Publishing
PO Box 152, Telford, Shropshire, England, TF2 2HA.

Dedicated to my wife
Rachel.

CONTENTS

INTRODUCTION

*Perhaps this is mine
Upon my sea of charm,
Written for no place in time,
But anywhere, under my arm.*

BEFORE I PRAY

The land quivered,
A mass of decaying flesh.
A mother knelt and prayed for
redemption,
And I watched her face,
It was white and dying,
It shed tears and pain
And I reminisce again.
I think of the screaming,
The blood and the exploding bodies.
I think of the mothers and children,
Dead and dying.
I think of the contorted bodies of the
soldiers
Caught in gesticulating death.
I think of the one that kneels before
me praying.
I kneel and pray!

BABE

Lying in a cot of gold
A little princess lies so bold.
The child of my royal queen,
A little babe, a mind so clean.

I PRAY

Please,
Please don't,
Please don't go.
Please don't go away,
Don't leave today
In any way.

HAIR

Stolen tales of lowland vales
And mountain slopes so fair
Could not describe or even bribe
The beauty in your hair.

RICHNESS

Fur coats and golden rings,
Delicate dresses and sapphire things,
And lots of other elegant pieces.
They don't really mean much!

DISPAIR

Sadness burns the face of love,
She doesn't really understand.
That poor girl that worships him,
He doesn't even hold her hand.

ALONE

There's a gentle touch of solitude
In the warmth of sunlight,
In the breath of a breeze,
In the quiet rustle of the oceans
waves upon the shore,
That gives a purely selfish pleasure
That can be indulged within
With no fear of reprise
Or expectations.

A MORNING PLAY

The sun was in the sky this morning
And a silky veil of white
Shrouded that blue sky
In anticipation.
The scent of spring was in the air
And a gentle, subtle breeze
Cleansed the breath of night
From the dew speckled fields.
Another day was spawned
For us to dance upon,
Beckoning us to portray our roles
Upon its open stage
Where every lover's story has been
told.
Ours is a fresh duet,
Never performed before,
But with shadows in the wings
To prompt the perfect score,
And as the spotlight
Shines from high
Upon the world,
I boldly proclaim
That I love you more
And more...
And more...

LOVE... WITHIN THE PAGES OF TIME

As the sun casts its first breath of
light upon the day
And the colours of the world come to
life,
A night time of loving has passed us
by,
Slipping into the pages of our
memories,
But this page has been written in
gold
To be bound with each tender touch
of our love,
Another page within the
enchantment of time
That will be recited in rhyme
To those who have dreamed of love.
We have found within ourselves
A love that casts us as one
And the passion of our bodies
embrace
Takes us to the meadows of pleasure
Where we walk and bathe in the joys
of our loving.
In the respite of that passion

14

We lie still within it's aura,
All words are full of inadequacies,
Even the vocabularies of Socrates
Could not enhance the depth of our
love,
In itself such a humble word to
describe an eternity of emotion,
Forever growing with the unrolling
Of the scrolls of our Souls.
To discover every rune on every
parchment of your being
Will cast an enchantment beyond the
powers of Merlin's alchemy
And I will stand with you till the
pages of time close,
Enraptured in our lovers ceremony.

ARE THERE CAR PARKS IN HEAVEN?

There's a market stall
In a local town
Every Saturday,
Weather permitting.
They stand,
With Christian intent,
To tempt our souls
With salvation.
Bookmarkers,
T-shirts, mugs
And baseball caps,
In contradiction
To their cause.
A Teddy bear,
Sash clad,
("Jesus loves you"),
Sits in proud posture,
King of the merchandise!
All at a righteous price!
Lace doilies and tablecloths,
Hand made toys
And other ploys
Enhance the tout
For funds.

Promises are sold,
With raffle tickets,
For a larger prize.
If your numbers up
You may take the ride.
"Holiday for two,
Can I tempt you?"
"Sorry."
I check the time.
"My meter's due!"

18

THE GIRL BY THE CROSS

Her face was hard and full of pain,
Her eyes wide and red.
She strains to look for a reason,
Her heart so dark and dead.

Night fell strong over the day,
And their cries ground the earth.
The shadows spread throughout the
land,
Death had shown it's worth.

The girl she stands and stares above,
The cross is tall and dark.
Her body sags upon its bones,
On Her God has left his mark.

Tears of blood flow from her eyes,
So black with pain and sorrow.
She'll never forget God's tortured Son,
He died to save tomorrow.

LEGENDS

We should walk the lands of the
ancient ones
To see what they once saw.
We should touch their minds with
ours
So we may learn some more.
We should stand inside their castles
And examine every stone.
We should clean the dust away
From what was once their home.
For
We cannot ask them questions.
We cannot touch their skin.
We cannot share their feelings.
And
We cannot feel their sin.
But
We can read the signs they left us
And colour between the lines,
We can understand their motives
And dig within their mines.
We can give their lives true meaning
If we care to take a look,
And ride their swans of glory
To write within their book.

A PICTURE

The road calls out to you like a siren,
Burning an image on your eyes,
An image that congeals around a
wound in your heart.
You run and you run but you don't
stop to look.
Chasing the shadows, wanting to
look.
Behind you is a picture painted on a
tarmac canvas,
With the blood from your mother's
face,
Edged with a lace of broken glass.
And your father no longer laughs.
You are suddenly reborn
To live up to scorn,
To live on with faith
Or die without hope.
Your age has no number...
You are instantly older...
And although the pain will last
forever
You'll survive,
You'll live on and strive...
Stand still!

Strong will!
Look up to the night,
Face the dawn of your parents' new
life,
Believe them gone to a new...
To live and watch over you.

THE ROOTS OF FEELINGS

Do?
Do You?
Do you dream?
Do you dream of tomorrow?
Do you count the stars like pearls?
Can you smell the scent of life on the
morning air?
Can you see the smile of nature on
the face of the sun?
Can you see the gentle look of
understanding in the eyes of the
Moon?
Have you cried?
Have you lain awake alone?
Have you dreaded the silence of
night?
Did you hear the rain beating heavy
on your window?
Did you feel the tears fall from the
heart of every lover hurt?
Did you pray for the eternal escape
of sleep and hide under the covers?
Would you cry?
Would you wonder why?

Would you dread the emptiness of
each day?
Could you hear the minutes of life
ticking slowly away?
Could you feel the cold darkness of
frosty winter mornings?
Could you see no purpose for the
daily chore of your existence?
I have felt!
I have felt all of this!
I have hurt every minute!
Now I hear the music in the
raindrops!
Now I see the colours of life in each
new leaf!
Now I see the fresh sparkle of day in
the surface of every puddle!
Each night I cherish!
Each quiet moment is warm!
Each touch is saturated with love!
Every kiss washes the darkness
away!
Every morning is the birth of a fresh
new day!
Every bird sings melodies in
harmony with my love!
And now I dream!

And I dream of tomorrow!
And I pray for each moment to last!
I can see the ecstasy of spring in each
flower!
I can hear life rustle in every branch
that dances the breeze!
I can smell the love of the world in
every breath of air that touches me!
Because I have felt, I know the worth
and the truth of our love!
Because I have felt, I appreciate the
richness of our time!
Because I have felt, I know the depth
of my love for you,
Rooted in my feelings,
In my heart and my soul!

ALIVE

I can hear their screams and shouts
And they become irritating
But when they are gone
Their echoes are exasperating.
The echoes shout in bouts
And madness walks in their shadow.
So beware
Of the hidden arrow
It will blind your soul and
awkwardness will prevail
Till you have battled all your Bears
And are left here in sorrow.
From that sorrow you must grow...
And reality be stronger than your
dreams
'Till you stand alone in life,
Secure!

<u>DREAM</u>

The boy stood alone,
Alone with his dream.
He held out his hand
But nothing was seen.
He called to his mother
And she turned his way,
But before she had seen him
The night drowned the day.
Alone in the darkness
He cried with his fear,
His only companion,
Along with the tear.
The tear that he cried
In his solitude.

27

LIQUID POWER

Do they realise?
Do they care?
Turning green,
Losing hair.
Liquid power
They devour,
Deaths sick disguise!
Punctured skin,
They push it in,
Fairy tales this death reveals,
Lust and pain it conceals.
Death comes close
A final dose
Quickly now,
Become death's ghost.

LISTEN

Come on,
Listen,
Listen to the day,
Listen to the morning.
Listen to the world,
Listen to it dawning.
It's the world of war-
Listen to them crying-
God knows what for!
Listen to them dying.
Come on,
Come and hear the noise,
Come and see the horror,
Come and hear their cries,
Come before tomorrow
When man has cleared the dead
away
And gives reasons for yesterday.
Come on!
Come and listen,
Listen to the bombs,
Listen to the people
As they leave their homes,
Listen to the children-
Listen to the children-

Listen to the children-
Standing by their mothers
Lying dead on the ground,
They have no others,
Watch them look around -
In innocence they cry,
They know not why
Their mothers lie dead,
They hurt no people-
They have no hatred,
But they are punished so-
Their sweet crying shows,
Listen!

MICKEY'S FUNERAL

Mickey Mouse is dead,
Donald's caught a cold,
Goofy shagged Snow White
While the Dwarves all dug for gold.
Heidi became a hooker
While Little Miss Muffet...
Pinocchio's now a transvestite
And Jiminy cuts and sniffs it.
Ms Blyton writes slash movies
While Gemima's on IVF
Toad's the pimp of his hall
And Badgers obsessed with himself.
In the corruption of the innocent
We devour our future dreams,
In contradiction of childhood
Confounded adult schemes!

TO HOLD A ROSE

Silently the roses
Form their gentle curves,
Shaping each petal
With loving care.
The perfect expression of beauty,
Subtle in their shadows,
Full of brilliant colour,
Flaming with passionate hues,
Tempting with their elegance.
They beckon you to take them in
your grasp
But sting you with your own
impatience.
To pluck a rose
And hold it in your heart,
You need the tender touch of a lover
And the patience of his love.

A LOST FRIEND

I did not know you well
But I knew you well enough
To know you
And to know that you
Were worth knowing,
Deserving to be known
As well as any one
Could be known.
Knowing you as I did
I know you will be missed
By those who knew you
For you knew us all well,
You took the time
To get to know us
I wish that I could have known you
more
Although I know
I will always treasure
Having known you.

For Paula

FROM BENEATH THE WIZARDS GOWN

Completely absorbed by the concept
of ego,
The wizardly elf stood alone by his
throne
Taller than the moon shadows
He had once looked up to.
He wore a gown to protect his soul
That was woven from the Runes of
Time.
The winds of the Earth Lords
Rippled the mysterious fabric
Causing star drops of meaning
To escape from beneath its heavy
hem.
The whirling words wandered the
ears of mortals,
Enchanting them with beguiling
images
From a magical world.
The wizardly elf was no longer alone
For his words had found friends.

WHO KILLED THE VIDEO STAR?

Tell me,

How far had you gone in life?
To the shops,
To the clinic,
Pre school jabs?
Not quite.
How many steps have you made in
life?
To play school?
I'm a cynic
You're still wet at night!

"Fuck you!"
They said when they
hit his head,
The plasma pumping
'till he was dead;
Then they scurried to
the shadows.
That night another
boy
Wet his bed!

"Oh no!"
A Dad cried to the
face that lied,
As the drama
unfolds, before they're
tried;
The Devil hurries for
his arrows,
In flight they hit,
Another died!

"Sod you!"
Cries made by the boy with the
blade
When he saw the
mess they'd made.
(At night he can see
old "Barrows"
Packed tight, bodies
Neatly laid.)

"So sorry."
Stars shone for all that
had gone
As well as the
bloodiest bloody one;
Many came to see the
horror,
In fright they left
Judging done!

"Fuck you!"
They yell, as they sit
in their cell
Debating if they are
truly in hell,
They think about
tomorrow,
Moon light, and the
toll
Of deaths' bell.

And so?

What have you done to earn your
fame?
Only two years
Have gone by
Since your dawn,
And yet
We all in this land know your
 name,
You can't even ask us why
You were born,
I bet!

 For James Bulger.

SEE WHAT THEY SAY
WE SEE, DO WE?

There's mashed potato in the sky
And puppets came from Mars
Disguised as Princes,
Their stories untold
Unfold in a child's eye.

Snow White is Lara Croft,
Hedge-hogs are now the stars,
Disguised as Princes
Battling the underworlds,
Their hardware never soft.

Cyber babes wearing tampons
Are dancing in our bars,
Disguised as Princes
In their Daddies' clothes,
Chics that should be capons.

TVs are our telephones
And horses now are cars,
Disguised as Princes
Of our endless roads,
But the cars have no bones.

Thoughts are bought and sold
And faces kept in jars
To disguise the Princes
Spinning in their lies,
Until the stories are all told!

Inspired by Emily, to the Ad men.

SHADOWS OF LIGHT

I've just seen a light,
A distant flicker from the past,
Casting shadows on tomorrow.
The light shone so brightly
yesterday,
And warmed me through to my soul
But then the curtains fell
And cast me into the darkness.
There is nothing but the shimmer of
candles now
And it is hard to see the doorway
Within so much darkness,
And I feel so cold,
The candles give me little warmth!
I seem to be fumbling
Within the shadows of the room,
Longing to walk out into the warmth
of the light,
But it's so hard to find the door
When so many shadows hide the
way.
Still I must remember
That around every shadow
There must be light,
Else the shadow would not exist!

Please open the curtains
To bathe us in daylight again.

TATTOO

Can anyone hear their cries?
The desperate emptiness of despair
That chimes loudly over the solitude.
Only darkness and silence can
compare
To the void of disillusionment that
plays with the betrayal.
Yet there is a passion within the
shadows,
Dancing within the nightmares,
Where reality toys with your soul
And coughs in embarrassment
At the games that are played.
The cries of the betrayers hang
heavy upon the air
As we watch with bewilderment
At the distorted illusions
And realise that our dreams
Are no more than dreams
And life *will* play us within its game!
Too tame we all are
For the Magician to fool foul
And the shadows of yesterday
Will throw darkness upon today.
Any hope we may have had

Of a rainbow's light
Will be washed away in the rain
Till the betrayal is complete
And they laugh beside their coffins of
deceit
'The Jesters of Dreams'
Tattooed upon their feet!

TERRORISM

Beside the gravestones shadows
stand,
Unseen in their twisted distortions,
Moving slowly as if to hide from the
suns eye.
Contorting their form as if in fright
Of being in sight.
As night-time approaches they join
hands
Dissolving into complete darkness
The unseen being seen as a whole,
No slice of light separating
These lonely memories of day.
Which way
Will they walk over the silent lands,
Onward toward the sinking star
Spreading the silencing of light
before them,
A marching army of silhouettes.
Fervent colours are on the run
From the gun
Of darkness as it brands
The day's domain with its mark.
The solidarity of solitude reigns
Over the fresh distractions of colour.

Daytime has been felled
And darkness upheld.
With confidence night stands
Tall and strong as the eyes of dawn
open.
Light is spawned from the flanks of
gloom,
Each shadows grip is torn from the
other
As a cavalry of light
Enters the fight,
Thrusting its strong bright bands
Between the scattering shadows.
Dispersing them with fresh dew drop
colours
Back to their hiding places
Behind each gravestone
Unseen...alone.

We need more light!

47

THE FUNERAL

One amongst a crowd of friends,
I'd come to say goodbye.
I would have liked to speak to you.
Overwhelmed by the reply
Of silence from your final bed,
I felt cheated
By your abrupt absence.
I was defeated
By my conscience to grieve.
I endured confusion,
Because although you were present,
It was an illusion
You were not there,
Despite the crowd of faces
Connected by your life,
There were no traces
Of you.
Your smell,
Your smile,
Your voice,
Your laughter,
Your ambition,
Your friendship,
Your compassion,
Your companionship,

Your passion,
Your love,
Your life.
Gone
You were.
Your presence in our past.
Memories in our future
Bound us there with you.
Each eye that cried had seen you,
Each heart that bled
Had loved you.
We are the chain of memories
That was your life,
Each link will go its way
Dispersed by your death
Held together finally
By your being there gone!

For Paula

SLEEPLESS

You can punch your pillows
And kick the quilt
You can share your night
And feel no guilt.
I love you when I hear your sighs
As the noisy night
Opens your eyes.
Being a part of you
Is the joy I feel
As you strop from the room
And my sleep you steel,
Even in your distain
I love you more,
As the smile on your lips
Comes through the door.
In the count of the days
My love still grows,
In the joy of your presence
My contentment shows
And in our closeness
Love has found a nest
Even if last night
Our eyes had no rest.

LA MER

Exotic...Erratic...Elastic in their
motion...
Too and fro,
Lost for a moment
As they just don't know.
Like people caught in the confusion
of a suburban nightmare,
They pass with despair,
Monotonous with strange grace,
Holding the golden glisten of light
upon their crests,
Rays that plant themselves so
confidently upon their soft surface.
...Still...yet they hold the hidden
anger of Neptune,
Rearing huge heads in fury like
white foaming stallions,
Pulsing with steaming blood
Pumped from the heart of hell,
Rising in the veins,
Swelling in the eyes,
Screaming as their hooves come
crashing to the sand,
And then, without a sound,
They pass on by...So sly.........the sea.

DANCING IN SATAN'S HALLS

Did Stanley Kubric say it first
When he wound that horrid orange?
Was it thrown away with Dracula's
soul
To the depths...out of range?
We saw Hitler dance with pungence
And slay Jews within its name,
We saw Sadam blaze his oily trail
Being in pretence of the game.
The seed it lives within our lands
It breeds within our dreams,
It coldly stole away our hands
And holds them where it means
Little to you and little to me,
We're lost upon its shore,
Can't lose it on a raging sea
We dare not know no more!
There's a bigger bounty at the gate
Where St Peter calls the last hand,
And it's dancing to Jagger's
sympathy,
Will there be a final stand?

THE PRICE OF A LIE

When I close my eyes at the end of
the day
My arms lying empty, no child to
hold,
I hide my heartache within my
dreams
Afraid to awake, as tomorrow
unfolds.
You're there in my dreams
You're there in my heart
But there's a distance between us
That keeps us apart.

The Sun breaks in chasing darkness
away
My heart is awoken, no sleep to hide
The memories I have, bright in my
mind,
I see your smile, your face full of
pride.
Your words in my mind
Your words in my soul
Have put mountains between us
That's taken a toll.

The day is passing, the Moon shines
the way,
I'm always your father, you my
child,
The time will come to make
memories again,
I'll see your smile, my heart running
wild.
Your love I'll regain
Your heart will return
And those forests between us
Will fire up and burn!

THE WISHING WELL

Into the dark hole
I peered,
A pit of dreams,
Tangled in the darkness.
A three-penny piece
From Granddad.
In the palm of my hand.
The end of my ninth summer
And I understood
The emptiness below,
A deep grave
Of wishes cast
With false expectations.
I made my wish
As the three-penny piece
Dissolved into the darkness.
Time walked by
Teasing and taunting
With glimpses of my dream
In a distant light,
But darkness prevailed.
I closed my eyes
To the falseness of my expectations,
Consoled to sleep without dreams,
No reward for my donation.

But then your gentle smile
Touched my eyes
Caressing them with your light,
The breath of your life
Refreshing my wish
And the truth of patience
Shining brightly in your eyes.
My dreams are replenished by your
touch,
They walk in the waking of day
With reality by their side
And I feel anointed by your love,
Blessed by the sacramental
Kiss of your heart.
Because I have seen the darkness
I recognised the purity of the light,
Your light,
Which has enlivened my heart.
You are my wish, my dream.

Into the daylight
I glance
A world of dreams
Unfolding in the brightness,
A three-penny piece
From Granddad
Cast into another land,

The start of a new summer
And I understand
The darkness behind
And now crave
The wish lasts
With full manifestations.

Three-pence well spent!

THE BEAUTY IN WAR

The sky darkened as the Sun lowered
its solemn head.
A mother's eyes watered and tears
fell like stones from her cheeks,
Her child of God lay dead!
Her hands crawled and caressed his
face,
Scratching the blood from his brow.
Her lips parted as she asked "Why? "
The pain in her voice brought tears
to the eyes of a soldier,
He stood in wonder
And groped for a reason in the mass
of bodies.
He dropped his gun,
Kicked it away from his view.
Then tore his green array from his
frame
And sank in disgrace and shame
That he was a worker of war.
A rat spluttered in a pool of blood,
An old man looked down, pain in his
face,
He stretched out his hand to touch
his leg......

It was gone!
He doubled up in pain
And vomited in the rain.
A small house erupted in flames of
red that polished
the face of the night,
And a young girl ran like a fireball,
She screamed and screamed till I
heard no more,
Then melted away in the heat.
I opened my eyes
And an old lady stood before me,
holding an arm in her hand,
She laughed
And blood flooded her mouth as she
too sank in pain.
I saw Christ floating in a black cloud,
His hair red and writhing in agony,
His hands outstretched,
Rusty bullets and bones penetrating
his thoughts
And death was pressing heavily on
his brow,
He cried!

THE OTHER WORLD.......REFLECTED

There's a world out there,
Not far beyond us
And,
As I sit alone to ponder,
Having wandered
Previously in that world,
I find that I like to be alone with you,
In our world.
Although I feel unattained,
Although I feel disabled,
I feel secure in your arms,
The warming glow of your embrace,
Of my embrace,
Of our embrace
Makes me safe
Within my place,
And with grace.
To our hearts alarms,
That which is fabled,
That which is ordained
Justly pearled,
As if in a glimpse of tender morning
dew
I was forever hurled,

Having pondered
But yet never to have wandered
Land
I would gladly cross
To be within you so fair.

To be within you so fair
I would gladly cross
Land,
But yet never to have wandered,
Having pondered,
I was forever hurled
As if in a glimpse of tender morning
dew,
Justly pearled.
That which is ordained,
That which is fabled,
To our hearts alarms
That, with grace,
Within any place
Makes me safe.
Of our embrace,
Of my embrace
The warming glow of your embrace,
I feel secure in your arms.
Although I feel disabled,
Although I feel unattained,

In our world
I find that I like to be alone with you,
Previously in that world
Having wandered.
As I sit alone to ponder
And,
Not far beyond us,
There's another world out there.

THOMAS JAMES WALKER

The dark light shaded upon the city
pathways.
The night echoed through the streets,
Subtly sighing to lost husbands and
business girls.
Shadows crept silently in shop
doorways
Where lovers made the nights last
stand,
And the timid girl moves his hand.
Family groups filter through,
Talking quietly about the latest West
End rage
As they stumble their way to a four
wheeled cage.
Children's hands clutch at mothers'
As their tenderness begins to show
And their tears begin to flow...
A father avoids Soho's flashing signs
And a tender wife calmly reminds
"It is getting late, our Thomas is
tired."
But Thomas is wide-awake
And hears each sound they secretly
make.

"Look at that slag!
Look at that whore!
Look at that sod on the floor!"
Thomas looks up and tries to see
more.
But with eyes glazed in innocence
All he sees are the coloured lights
As they bounce through the rain
drops,
Clinging to the cold glass,
And his finger draws a smiley face
In the steam of his breath.

WALKING

Walking –
First with my right foot
Then with my left,
Patiently timing each step,
Alongside the walls of the castle,
Looking up at those silent walls,
Sculpted by the rain,
As it trickles down them – on route
to the drain.
It will take these fragments of stone
Far from their home,
Where no one will know their origin.

Left foot – right foot – left foot – right
foot –

As I walk on past the drain
The trickles plague my brain.
Do they take footsteps?
Do they time their trickles?
Do they rebuild the walls in distant
waterfalls?
(A natural Altar)
How do they wander?
How do they flow?

Where do they go?
Sinking deep underground
Hiding away the history they've
found.
Electrons, protons and neutrons
Linking atomic theory
To this castles story.
The trickles take away
The history that has lain so still
For many a day,
For so many years,
Seen death in so many fears.
Felt blood trickle down its surface,
Trickles to the drain
By my feet,

Left foot...right foot...left foot...right
foot...

Walking.........

A DAY ON THE BEACH OF WAR

Soft and dry,
The sand is warm under foot,
Each step sinks like broken dreams
And there are many footsteps behind
them.
This hot sand rubs between the toes
And scratches under the eyelids.
Lips are dry,
Closed tight against the desert dust,
Salty sweat drips from each nose,
Each armpit and groin is drowning
with heat.
No body, today, will be kissed or
caressed
By more than a bullet or a memory.
Tears they cry
For each dream left behind.
Each parent, spouse and child
spawned
Dance profoundly in their hearts
and thoughts.
Hearts pounding with the drum beat
of fear
Veins pulsing with rivers of
adrenaline.

Shots will fly
Through the dense desert storm,
Blood will flow onto the desert land
And life will slowly drain through
every grain,
No castles will be built in this moist
sand.

ANONYMOUSLY LOST

In the dark shadow a face is lost,
Pale with sickness, scared with time,
Eyes drawn tight against a red web
of sleep...
Corrupted by synthetic whores
Standing begging by old pub doors,
Painted with false smiles that
cracked in scented isles of frustrated
youth.
Seven years of catching cold,
Hoarding thoughts of gaining gold.
Walking out in the city drag,
With your well trained arm
And your sacred charm
You swung your plastic bag.
Are you that girl the papers said
Was lost in confusion and now
thought dead,
Or just some sin from a city slum
Who has lost the taste for chewing
gum?
You're not so old,
But pertaining to a life that is
bought and sold

You've gained age with perfumed
soil.
The epic life you planned and
quested...burnt away.
In a shop doorway, injected and
infested...life drips by,
Even your plastic Mac has lost its'
lie,
Still your blood filled mouth sighs
goodbye...

YOUR DREAM

Did the vampires catch you
As they trespassed within your
dreams?
I stood there and watched you,
As you twitched within their
temptations,
But you rejected me,
As you often do,
And the rescue was your loneliness.
Yet today's dance will be yours
For you know that I follow your
steps.
And I will always be there,
Despite your recoils
And you may disguise your
intentions
Within my dreams
But you fool not the fool
For I am not that jester
And the foil is unsheathed.
And I am still alone
In my solitude.

DOUBLE O CLOWN

Tomorrow there will be a clown
Who will jest and cry from plastic
roses,
He'll stamp on your toe
And dislocate at twenty paces.
He'll bounce his nose
In various hollows of amusement,
All with his coloured array of tears;
Sometimes more real than his own.
Before the show goes on
He will sit all alone
Disguising his solemn face.
Why a fool?
Why a jester?
Why the tool of laughter?
In the ring
The cries circle his mind,
Climbing high
Then swooping to his ears,
Scratching at his innocence
Like vamporous teeth
Pushing apart the living cells of flesh,
Plunging deep into the plasmic
oceans
To draw from his heart

Every pulse of life.
He will tentatively dance
Along the sawdust carpeted stage,
The idiot idol,
Masquerading his foolery,
Wearing stupidity
Like fake jewellery.
Everyone is his friend
But no one loves the fool.

Tomorrow there would have been a
clown,
But after contemplation,
He decided to become a secret agent
And endeavours to keep his secrets
Between himself and the fool.

THE TRUTH

Once upon a time
You would dream your dreams aloud
And the stories,
Which they told,
Would surround you.
But now it seems
That reality's supreme
And the harshness of true life
confounds you.

THE LAST DAY
(A DAY IN THE LIFE OF A DEAD MAN)

He woke this morning full of dread,
Stumbled loosely out of bed.
Put his pants on back to front,
Performed an acrobatic stunt,
Tore a button from his shirt,
Tripped over madam's skirt,
Broke a lace from his shoe,
Lost his wallet down the loo.
Mumbled slowly down the stairs,
Found his wife among some hairs,
He asked her why he was so late,
She said it was the devil's bate.
The days to young to understand,
He dropped a knife and cut his hand.
She said he'd come home late last
night
And killed the cat in a fight.
He moaned away the sound she
made
And wondered about his razor blade,
Yesterday it cut like fire,
Now it seems to be a liar,

77

Cuts around his beard and through
his skin.
The frying pan makes a din!
He looks in anger at the stove,
His wife asks how he drove!
In such a state he'd surely crash!
She moans about the household cash.
He dries his face upon the towel,
The dog lets out a howl,
"You're standing on it's foot you
fool!"
The kids pass by in rush for school.
'I wish to God she'd take the pill'
His wife- her tongue is flapping still,
The breakfast waits upon the table,
She moans about his jacket label,
It's not the one he had before
And what is that thing on the floor...
The bill that paid for the night just
past,
How long could this nagging last?
As he leaves his meal
In search of peace to steal
And escapes through the door...
He wonders what it has all been for?
They shared happiness once
Exchanging love with every glance,

Debating schemes,
Entwining dreams,
Making plans,
Holding hands...

His car it waits upon the road
To carry his unhappy load...
Through traffic lights of red and
green
He recollects the night he'd seen.
He's trucking through the city dawn,
Right now he wished he wasn't born.
A screech of brakes, a crunch of steel,
The pain and blood are truly real!
He's carried off in a motorised bed
The day not passed, a man is dead!

DELIGHT

You caress my life
With a touch as soft as Venetian silk
And as pure as freshly fallen artic snow.
Each morning you breathe life into my soul,
And I awake within a dream,
All nightmares cast aside.
I ride upon a Unicorn of delight,
Its silver winged plumage
Shining as a thousand stars
In the sunlight of your eyes.
Each glance you cast
Dazzles me with love
And I hold your face,
As gentle as a dove
In the memory of my vision,
To guide me through the day
Till you lay beside me again
As the eyes of the world close to the night
And we are enraptured within our love.

METAPHYSICAL LOVERS

Angels in the dark sky,
Shining like nightmares
In the tear of my eye.
I call your names,
Play your games
And lose...then pretend.
I cry another nightmare
Sit
Stand
Walk and stare
Pray and glare.
Then drips another tear!

Contraceptive lovers,
Capitulate devils,
Cry-
Die-
Live in hell,
Flee from my dell.
Hide your gordy faces
Lose your stumbling images,
Cry in your pits of shame
For with you lies the blame!

MORE SERENE DREAMS, PLEASE

When I look at you sleep,
Your eyes closed,
Face relaxed,
Your mouth so still,
The moonlight touching your golden
hair
Draped over your pillow,
As if cast by the breath of a fairy
prince,
My mind wanders...
Not aimlessly
But to your future...
What will it hold?
You are my princess,
My child,
My angel,
As every daughter is
To even the most wild.

I look at your face in sleep,
So small,
So white,
So gentle,
So sweet,
So fragile,

Like porcelain,
Yet so warm with life.
How can I send you into the world?
The world of hate,
Of money,
Of vice,
Of violence.
You are my child,
My princess...

***

Let's take a walk,
Follow my steps.
See the men
Pissed and brainless,
How and why
Did their minds die!

Wait! Look!
In the shadows,
Who is she?
Legs so long,
Blouse so tight,
So sexy,
But look closer!
A tattoo on her neck,

A scar on the cheek,
The smell of her breath.
'Lookin' for business luv?'
Matted hair,
Poorly scented armpits
And groin no doubt!

Did someone mention love?
Pretty girl,
Could have been or was,
Yet well worn,
Shop soiled and torn,
Nearly new,
Just a thousand previous owners
(For a few minutes a time).
Oh how sublime!
What hurts,
What cuts so deep,
What tears my soul
And sheds my sleep,
Is that once
In some morning dew,
She was someone's princess too!

A warning to my daughters.

FOUL FATE

His youth was one with the glows of
sadistic joy.
His mind was layered with blood and
fingers
From a poor distorted soul.
His memory sits on death, smells and
lingers
While his body rots so foul.
For he lived so long ago
And killed so far away,
But to this day
His heart has lay
In the stench of his bloody deeds.
`Till Earth has stopped
And time is still,
His guilt is with God alone,
For no man knows where the ripper
lies!

ONLY

A grey beard hangs like a dying leaf
to his face,
His skin well worn with age,
His life slipping by with little grace
And his thoughts are solemn, free
from rage.
He is only an old tramp,
No one cares about his aching head
Or his dirty clothes, torn and damp,
Nor where tonight he'll make his bed.
" He is only a tramp" they'll say
And they'll pass him off for another
day.
He is only a blind tramp but he sees
all,
He senses the anger in your face
And he can see in your heart
The way you look with disgrace
At his battered array,
He may warn you some day
But until then he'll leave you alone,
Knowing behind his unseeing eyes,
That some day you will find your
true home
Or be yourself, despised.

NEW YEAR

Big Ben chimes to the world,
His timeless voice calling to us all
As the last seconds of the past year
slip by,
He laments the birth of times new
page.
His song discards the wrongs dealt
In the last dozen moon dances
And rejoices the joys, cast in
memories,
Gilt inlaid in our minds,
To relish forever.
The silence that follows his last toll,
Celebrates our pathway
Through the New Year ahead
And the page he leaves us
Is for our delight to scribe upon
As we will.
His last word is the cue
For our first
And the future is ours,
And that is the point of the toast we
raise...
It is in respect of our future
memories.

THE PEBBLE MAN

A man of old walked on the shore,
His hat and cane in hand,
He softly bent and picked a pebble
Up from the sand.
He looked and gazed upon the stone
And wondered why it was
This pebble lay here, by the shore,
I heard him say "Because".
"Because it's here and not there,
A reason better than most.
Will no one tell me why this stone
Lies out here on the coast?"
He raised his hand and threw it
hard,
It skimmed along the water.
His hat and cane in hand
He bent, then threw another.

I AM, I THINK. WHO AM I?

Oh how strange
That we are never who we think we
are.
We typecast our personalities
In the daydreams of our fantasies,
Walking on through to reality,
Albeit subconscious in our
wandering.
Our maturity comes with the
realisation
That we are not who we want to be
But who we are.

THE ENDING

A city caught in the misty drag
of a slow timeless death.
A lonely whore caught on the edge
of a long ending breath.
Symbols of a civil world!
Symbols of the Devils' poem!
Endings to a tunnelled fate!

And here stands the whore,
Here stands the prostitute of Satan,
Here in a dream of boredom,
Selling out for luxury and science.
Here - before our eyes - is the ending,
The path that leads to the edge of the
Cliff

And......then...

An empty Page for the future... TS